AMELIA
EARHART

Every effort has been made to ensure historical accuracy. Some facts herein differ
from Earhart's own, widely acknowledged accounts.

Tanaka, Shelley.
Amelia Earhart: the legend of the lost aviator / by Shelley Tanaka; illustrated by David Craig.
   p. cm.
1. Earhart, Amelia, 1897–1937—Juvenile literature. 2. Women air pilots—United States—
Biography—Juvenile literature.
3. Air pilots—United States—Biography—Juvenile literature. I. Title.

TL540.E3T36 2008
629.13092—dc22
[B]
2007039749

ISBN: 978-0-8109-7095-3

Printed and bound in Singapore
10 9 8 7 6 5 4 3 2 1

HNA
harry n. abrams, inc.
a subsidiary of La Martinière Groupe
115 West 18th Street
New York, NY 10011
www.hnabooks.com

Produced by
Madison Press Books
1000 Yonge Street, Suite 200
Toronto, Ontario
Canada M4W 2K2
madisonpressbooks.com

AMELIA EARHART

The Legend of the Lost Aviator

By SHELLEY TANAKA

Illustrated by DAVID CRAIG

A MADISON PRESS BOOK

ABRAMS BOOKS FOR YOUNG READERS, NEW YORK

GROWING UP

Amelia Earhart remembered seeing her first airplane when she was eleven years old. She was visiting the Iowa State Fair—in 1908 it was already one of the biggest in the country. The midway echoed with shrieks from the Ferris wheel and the roller coaster. Smells mingled from the livestock building and the lunch stands. There were moving picture shows, horse races, dairy cow contests, family picnics. Everyone was dressed up in hats and jackets and long dresses, even though it was a hot summer day.

Amelia and her younger sister, Muriel, were led from one display to another—endless rows of farm animals, vegetables, flowers, farm machines.

Set off to one side was what looked like a heap of rusty wire and wood. It was an airplane.

"Look, dear, it flies," one of the adults said.

Amelia was not impressed. She was too busy admiring her prize purchase. It was a hat made from an upside-down peach basket, and she had just bought it for fifteen cents.

Life in those days was interesting enough without airplanes. There was school, of course, but Amelia was a good student, and there was always time left over for fun. She loved to read, especially adventure stories. When she and Muriel were given chores, they would take turns reading out loud while the other worked.

Amelia spent much of grade school living in her grandparents' big house in Atchison, Kansas. It had a library, a piano, and a yard with a barn. Amelia's mother made her daughters bloomered gym suits so they didn't have to play in skirts like other girls at that time. Amelia and Muriel rode

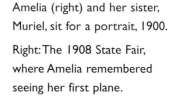

Amelia (right) and her sister, Muriel, sit for a portrait, 1900.

Right: The 1908 State Fair, where Amelia remembered seeing her first plane.

4

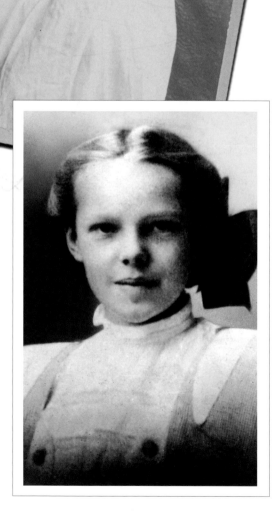

Amelia as an infant,
circa 1897.

horses, played basketball and tennis, went bike riding, and had mudball fights. They asked for, and got, footballs for Christmas.

But even better than the usual sports and games were the adventures and experiments that the sisters got up to on their own. They explored the sandstone bluffs and caves along the muddy Missouri River. They spent hours poring over their grandparents' maps and atlases. Then the girls would climb aboard an old wrecked carriage that sat in the barn and go on pretend journeys. Africa was a favorite destination. The place names were deliciously mysterious—Senegal, Timbuktu, Khartoum. In their imagination they traveled along mighty rivers and crossed jungles and deserts, just like the explorers they learned about in school.

They built a brick oven so they could fry eggs and "invent" new recipes. When Amelia learned in Sunday school about the manna that fell from heaven to feed the children of Israel, she decided to try to make some herself. She imagined manna would look like a little white muffin, and that it would taste like a delicious combination of angel food cake and a popover. She never quite perfected the recipe, but she spent a lot of energy—and flour and sugar—trying.

Amelia as a young girl, 1904.

Amelia always liked to try new things, "first-time things." And she loved to make things go. She would go sledding down steep icy hills lying flat on her stomach, which wasn't considered proper for girls, but the ride was faster and more thrilling that way. After seeing her first "rolly coaster" when she was seven, she built her own in the backyard using long planks propped against the roof of the tool shed.

Life was sweet in those early years. Amelia grew up thinking that girls could accomplish as much as boys, and that the world was a place full of wonder and adventure.

Amelia's childhood home
in Atchison, Kansas.

Air Travel—the Coming Thing

Amelia Earhart remembered seeing her first plane in 1908, only five years after Wilbur and Orville Wright invented the airplane that made their famous flight at Kitty Hawk. But during her lifetime, air travel advanced enormously. By the late 1920s the first passenger planes had appeared. They were small, noisy, and smelly (the combination of gasoline fumes and the disinfectant used to clean up after airsick passengers!). The ride was often bumpy because the planes could not fly very high.

Throughout the 1930s, air travel became more comfortable. Passenger planes were bigger and better ventilated. Planes could fly higher, so the ride was smoother. Soft seats, onboard snacks, and flight attendants also helped.

By 1937, more than one million people were traveling by plane in the United States each year.

A Farman, one of the earliest planes, circa 1908.

FIRST FLIGHT

Amelia's early childhood was filled with good times. High school was a different story. Her beloved grandmother died. From time to time her father drank heavily, and he often had to change jobs. The family moved a lot, and Amelia ended up going to six high schools before she graduated. She later said that all that moving around gave her a taste for traveling to new places and meeting new people, but it was not an easy time. Over the next several years her parents split up, got back together, and eventually split up for good. Meanwhile the girls headed off to college—Muriel to Toronto, and Amelia to a school near Philadelphia.

In 1917 Amelia decided to spend Christmas visiting her sister in Toronto. World War I was coming to an end, and the wounded were returning from the battlefields in droves.

One wintry day she saw four men on crutches struggling to walk down the street together. Suddenly, being useful seemed more important than going to college. So Amelia moved to Toronto to work as a nurse's aide. She scrubbed floors, made beds, rubbed backs. She served endless bowls of rice pudding to the wounded—food so unappetizing that some puddings came back uneaten and marked with little crosses and the inscription RIP. When the flu epidemic struck in 1918, she worked even longer hours in over-crowded wards.

But there were bright spots, too. The need for combat planes in World War I meant governments were quickly developing better planes and training new pilots to fly them. That winter Amelia visited a military flying field. The runway was noisy, windy, and cold. The pilots had to smear their faces with grease to keep their skin from freezing.

Shortly before her twenty-fourth birthday, Amelia bought herself a Kinner Airster, which she called the Canary.

One day, as she stood watching the planes, and the propellers blew snow in her face, she felt an urge to fly. Perhaps flying, she thought, would be one of the few worthwhile things to come out of the war.

When the war ended, Amelia returned to the United States and tried to decide what to do with her life. For a time she enrolled in medical school, doing the "peculiar things" people did to become doctors. She fed orange juice to mice and dissected cockroaches, which, she discovered, had surprisingly large brains. At one point she took a course in automobile repair. Her parents moved to California and tried to rebuild their shaky marriage, and they convinced Amelia to join them.

But she didn't forget airplanes.

In 1920, she went to an air show near Los Angeles with her father.

"Dad, you know, I think I'd like to fly," she said suddenly. She convinced him to ask about going up in a plane because she was too shy to ask herself. Her father agreed. He was sure that one ride would be enough to cure her of her crazy idea.

The engine roared loudly as the plane rose into the air. Soon she could see the ocean. It didn't even feel as if they were going very fast, yet before she knew it they were landing.

She was hooked.

Flying lessons were incredibly expensive. Besides, this was a time when most people thought a woman's place was in the home, and that dangerous activities should be left to the men. Still, Amelia was determined. She even found a woman instructor, Neta Snook, who believed that women could fly as well as men.

Amelia soon learned that flying was a little more complicated than driving a car. Keeping the wings level was difficult at first, because if you tried too hard the plane wobbled. She learned how to turn and—trickiest of all—how to land.

Right: Amelia's graduation photo from a prep school in Philadelphia, Pennsylvania, circa 1918.

Below: Amelia before her first flying lesson with instructor Neta Snook at Kinner Airfield, January 3, 1921.

Other Women Fliers

Amelia Earhart may be the most famous female pilot in history, but she was by no means the first. Harriet Quimby, America's first licensed woman pilot, became the first woman to fly across the English Channel, in 1912. Amelia later said that Quimby's hour-long solo flight through dense fog required more bravery and skill than her own solo flight across the Atlantic in 1932.

In the early 1920s, women also performed airborne stunts at county fairs and exhibitions. And in 1930, seven years before Amelia's last flight, Englishwoman Amy Johnson became the first woman to fly solo halfway around the world—from England to Australia.

During World War II, women pilots in Great Britain, the United States, and Germany tested warplanes and delivered them from the factories to the airfields, and in Russia, women even flew fighter planes in combat.

Harriet Quimby, the first woman to fly across the English Channel, sits in her plane, 1912.

However, she wanted to be able to do more than take a plane up and down. Straight flying, like straight driving, was simple enough. It was being able to get out of tough situations that counted. So she learned how to "play around" in the air—how to dive, roll over, spiral down in a tailspin.

Amelia had taken flying lessons for a grand total of two and half hours when she decided that life would not be complete unless she owned her own plane. She wanted one of the new, snappy little "sport" planes. They could take off more quickly, climb more steeply, and fly faster than Neta's clunky old Canuck war plane.

Flying a light plane was also tricky—like flying a leaf in the air, Neta Snook once said. It came down for a landing quickly, and the smallest crosswind could send it skidding.

Amelia didn't care. She bought a bright yellow Kinner Airster. The propeller blades were no higher than her armpits, and the plane was so light that she could drag it around the airfield by its tail!

The Kinner cost twice as much as a used Canuck, so from then on, Amelia would have to work—sometimes at more than one job at a time—to pay for her flying. On weekends she would take the streetcar to the end of the line and then walk several miles to the airport.

Once she took off in good weather and headed up to see what her engine could do at higher altitudes. She ran into dense fog. It was a very strange feeling because her plane had no instruments that told a pilot which way was up.

You only knew you were upside down when your feet dropped off the rudders and your seatbelt tightened!

Amelia decided she'd better come down as quickly as possible. So she put the plane into a tailspin until she emerged from the fog, and then landed.

One of the old-timers on the ground was not impressed.

"Suppose the fog had lasted all the way to the ground?" he asked.

Flying was a risky business. She crashed, more than once. One time the motor cut out just after takeoff and she landed in a cabbage patch and bit her tongue. Another time she came down in a muddy field where the wheels stuck and the plane tipped over. Once she landed in a soft bed of tall weeds that stopped the plane so suddenly that it flipped over, broke her seatbelt, and threw her out.

None of these "little crack ups" dampened her love of flying.

Amelia had to find a way to support herself and her expensive hobby. After many false starts—filing for a telephone company, taking photographs, driving a gravel truck, teaching English—she finally found a job she liked. She became a social worker. And for a time, flying took a backseat to earning a living.

Amelia beside her plane in 1928.

13

THE *FRIENDSHIP*

Amelia was working in Boston in April 1928 when the phone call came. She was a social worker at a center that helped immigrant families settle into their new lives. She loved her job, especially being with children. She took them for rides in her bright yellow car. For some it was their first car ride ever.

She broke away from a noisy crowd of children who were piling in for after-school activities to take the call. On the other end of the line a voice asked whether she was interested in doing something dangerous in the air.

It turned out that a publisher and promoter named George Putnam was looking for a woman who was willing to fly from Trepassey, Newfoundland to Southampton, England. Amelia would not fly the plane herself. All she had to do was go along for the ride. But, if the flight was successful, she would be the very first woman to fly across the Atlantic Ocean.

Such a flight was indeed dangerous. In the previous year nineteen people, including two women passengers, had died trying to cross the Atlantic by air.

Was she willing to take the risk?

The answer was yes.

The entire project was filled with delays and difficulties due to poor weather conditions. Three times a tugboat took the crew out to the pontoon plane—the *Friendship*—anchored in Boston Harbor (too many good-byes and too little going, Amelia thought), before they finally took to the air. A few minutes after takeoff the cabin door slid open. Amelia, sitting behind the cockpit with the extra fuel, dived for a gasoline can that was edging toward the opening. She nearly fell out of the plane.

Amelia flies across the Atlantic in the *Friendship*.

14

At the edge of the Atlantic in Trepassey, Newfoundland, they waited thirteen days for rain and fog to clear, and for the wind to be right. And once again it took three tries before they got off—after leaving every spare ounce of weight behind, including seat cushions, all their personal luggage, and their backup gasoline. They also left behind their life jackets and a rubber dinghy, even though if anything went wrong, they might have to land in the middle of the ocean. They did carry a few sandwiches, as well as extra drinking water and pemmican—a paste made of dried meat and melted fat that could, in theory, keep them alive for several days. Amelia was told the explorers had carried pemmican to keep them healthy and happy, though she had her doubts. To her the stuff looked like "cold lard with dark unidentified lumps floating in it."

In any case, she was too excited to eat during most of the flight. While pilot Wilmer "Bill" Stultz and mechanic Louis "Slim" Gordon took care of the actual flying, Amelia spent much of the time kneeling in front of the navigator's chart table looking out the window.

Later she would describe the flight as a "voyage in the clouds."

A crowd gathers at Trepassey Bay, Newfoundland, to watch Amelia and the rest of the *Friendship* crew take off on their transatlantic flight.

Whenever she flew, she never got tired of watching clouds. When you were inside them they were clammy and gray, but from a distance they took on strange and fantastic shapes of all kinds. Some were like "shimmering veils," and some looked like icebergs, or caves, or castles. Some "reared their heads like dragons," and some were piled high like "gobs of mashed potatoes." Others were fluffy like "little lambs" or "white scrambled eggs."

And when the sun set, the highest peaks were tinted pink, showing shadowy gray hollows beneath. Watching them was like "gulping beauty," she wrote.

They flew into the night. Amelia ate an orange and tried to write in the logbook in the blackness, using her left thumb to try to keep her pencil going in a straight line.

But when dawn broke, things were not going well. The left engine was coughing. The radio was dead. Worst of all, they had only an hour's supply of gas left. They should have reached land long ago.

Suddenly they spotted a transport steamer in the distance, and they headed toward it. But with a dead radio there was no way to communicate with the ship to find out where they were. Amelia scribbled a note asking the steamer to paint its position on its deck. Then she tied the note in a bag, along with a couple of oranges for weight.

As the plane circled, she dropped the bag through the hatch—only to watch the wind carry her little "bomb" far away.

Dear Miss Earhart…

Amelia Earhart received lots of fan mail, including letters from children who wanted to know about flying. Some asked technical questions ("Why is the monoplane faster than the biplane?"). Some wanted to go with her on her world flight ("I am fifteen years old, 105 pounds, quiet, and want to see the world. I have no money, but will work my head off…"). Some wanted to learn how to fly ("Please teach me to fly… I will repay you if it takes the rest of my life…I haven't got much because my father loads coal in a mine").

And some just wanted her to know how much they admired her ("Behind the brick plant near our home there is a beautiful little lake with blueish water so I named it 'Lake Amelia.'…I adopted 'Amelia' as my middle name …I would have named my duck Amelia but since it is a he duck I can't").

The trio in the *Friendship* didn't know what to do. Should they land in the ocean and let the ship pick them up? Or should they carry on, in the hope that they must be close to reaching their goal?

They decided to carry on.

Finally, after flying for more than twenty hours since takeoff, Slim spotted a blue shadow growing out of the mists. He stopped chewing his scrambled egg sandwich and studied the mound for several moments. Was it just another bank of fog?

Suddenly he yelled out. His sandwich went flying out the window.

It was land.

Amelia looks out of the
Friendship after their arrival.

In fact, the *Friendship* had missed Southampton completely and ended up landing in Wales. But they had made it across the ocean, and now Amelia was famous. She insisted that Bill and Slim had done all the work, and that she had simply sat in the plane like a "sack of potatoes." It didn't matter. She was the first woman to fly across the Atlantic. She was a star. And in a way, her work was just beginning.

Crowds gathered wherever she went. She received endless bouquets of flowers. When people learned that she had left all her luggage behind, she was given free shopping sprees. (She arrived in Europe with two scarves, a comb, and a toothbrush, but returned to the United States by ship with three trunks filled with clothes and gifts.)

In America, there were receptions, marching bands, medals, and interviews. Everyone wanted her photograph and her autograph. In New York City, Amelia, Bill, and Slim rode in a parade to City Hall while people cheered and showered them with confetti. She was asked to write articles and give countless speeches telling the world about aviation.

By the late 1920s, airplanes were no longer the rare sights they had been when Amelia was a child. Around the world, planes carried passengers, mail, and freight every day. But most people still considered flying to be dangerous and unnatural. Amelia wanted to convince them otherwise.

Everywhere she went, she described what it felt like to fly to

Amelia poses for photographs with *Friendship* pilot Wilmer "Bill" Stultz (right) and mechanic Louis "Slim" Gordon.

people who had never done it. Because a plane was not connected to the ground, she explained, it did not make you dizzy like riding a roller coaster or peering over the edge of a tall building. You did not even feel as if you were moving particularly fast. There were no telephone poles or trees whipping by to give you a sense of speed, the way there were on a highway. And coming in for a landing felt like less of a drop than riding down an elevator.

Amelia explained how air flowed like liquid, and how it was pushed up when it hit a clump of trees or a mountain. If a plane hit this mass of air, it would be tossed just like a boat on a wave. So that they could get a sense of what it was like to fly through thick fog, she encouraged people to try walking in a straight line while blindfolded.

But mostly she described the joy of flying. How you sometimes felt as if you could see the whole world. Even mighty mountains looked humble from the air, she said. Trees looked like bushes. She described sneaking beneath the clouds and playing hide-and-seek with the sun. The fun of scattering a small cloud by diving into it.

And she spoke out on behalf of girls and women becoming fliers—or anything else they wanted.

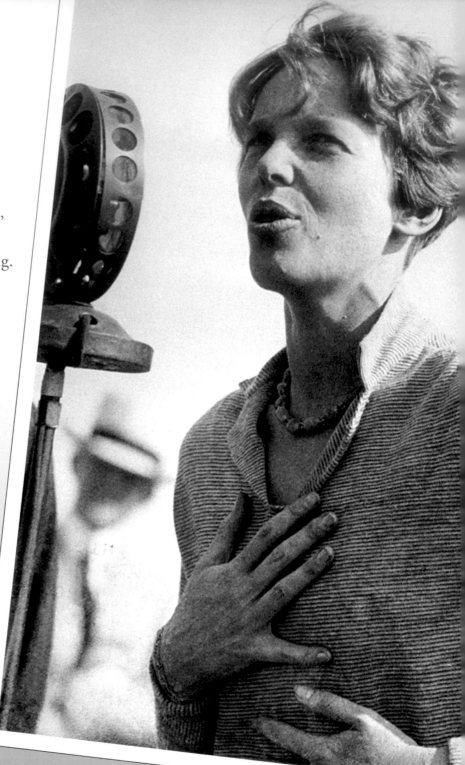

Amelia gives a speech about the *Friendship*'s transatlantic flight, July 11, 1929.

20

Amelia married George
Putnam in 1931.

"You're saying that women are or should
be the equal of men in aviation?" a cranky male
journalist asked her once.

"No, not in aviation," Amelia replied. "In
everything."

She became president of the Ninety-Nines,
the first organization of licensed women pilots.
She helped to start up two commercial airlines,
handling passenger complaints and dealing
with the problems that were constantly cropping
up in this brand-new industry. Once she had
to figure out how to transport a pony in the
passenger compartment. (He was sold two seats,
though he still had to stand partly in the aisle!)

Her writing and lecture tours made Amelia
more famous than ever. She received bags full of fan mail. Babies were
named after her. She even received proposals of marriage, though she didn't
need them. In 1931 she married George Putnam, who became her partner
and supporter in all her projects.

Amelia was very busy, but not too busy to make time for flying. She
got her transport pilot's license—one of only seven women at that time.
She became the first woman to fly solo across the United States from the
Atlantic to the Pacific and back. She set women's speed and altitude records.

Oddly, she received a lot of attention for what she called stunt flying—
flying farther, higher, faster—when she really just wanted people to think
of flying as boringly normal. She dreamed of the day when traveling by air
would be as common as driving a car, and flying would be just an everyday
way of getting from one place to another.

GOING SOLO

Amelia was famous for being a passenger on the *Friendship*. Now she wanted to try to fly across the Atlantic herself. In her own plane. Alone.

No one had flown the Atlantic solo since Charles Lindbergh in 1927. Two women pilots had tried to make the crossing and had failed. Amelia reckoned her chances of succeeding were one in ten.

It was dangerous. But she wanted to prove to herself, and to anyone else who was interested, that an experienced woman pilot could do it. That *she* could do it.

So she set about getting her new plane—a bright red Lockheed Vega—ready to go. The plane's wooden fuselage was strengthened, and a 500-horsepower engine was installed. Instruments were added, including three new compasses. Additional tanks were put in the wings and cabin to hold extra fuel—more than enough to get her across the Atlantic, if she flew in a straight line.

The cockpit was a cozy cubbyhole with everything within reach, from her thermos of hot chocolate to extra fuses. On her left were two pump handles that allowed her to change fuel from one set of tanks to another. If the motor-driven pump failed, she would have to pump by hand.

Whenever she could, she took the Vega up in the air. She practiced blind flying—flying without looking out the cockpit window and using only her instruments—to get used to the black, foggy, and stormy conditions she might meet over the Atlantic.

By the third week of May 1932, the plane was ready to go. Amelia began to watch the weather closely. She remembered too well the long delay at Trepassey during the *Friendship* flight. She knew that bad weather in the eastern Atlantic could hang around for many days.

Amelia crosses the Atlantic in her Lockheed Vega, becoming the first woman to complete a solo transatlantic flight.

Flight Delayed... Again

Modern airports are busy around the clock. Pilots are guided by computers, and runways are brightly lit. Planes take off and land day and night, in all but the most icy or stormy conditions.

But in Amelia's day, flight delays were common. Mechanical breakdowns were routine. At the smallest landing strips, refueling was slow, since gasoline had to be pumped from the barrels by hand.

A pilot had to wait for acceptable weather all along the route, and the wind direction had to be right for takeoff. (Planes get better lift if they take off into a slight headwind, which allows them to climb higher, faster—the same reason you run into the wind to lift a kite into the air.)

And not just any time of day would do. Takeoff conditions were often best in the morning, when the air was cooler and denser, which helped to lift the plane. Schedules also had to be timed so a plane would reach its destination during daylight, when the runway and surrounding landmarks could be clearly seen.

On the morning of May 20, the phone rang at the hangar in New Jersey. The weather in Newfoundland was perfect. She should leave right away.

After an overnight stop in New Brunswick, she reached Harbour Grace, Newfoundland. The weather was no longer quite perfect, but she could leave that evening. She read a final message from George before shaking hands with her mechanics and climbing into the cockpit. The wind was blowing right into the face of the plane—perfect for takeoff. Amelia pushed the throttle forward to make the airplane go faster. She could feel the tail come up and the plane get lighter and lighter on the wheels. The Vega gathered speed and rose into the air easily despite the heavy load.

For several hours everything was fine. The weather was fair as she flew with the sunset at her back. The moon came up, and that was a comfort. The moon and the stars were always friendly beacons to a pilot flying through the night.

Suddenly, something happened that had never occurred in all her years
of flying. Her altimeter—the instrument that measures height above the
ground—stopped working. The hands flopped uselessly around the dial.

Then the moon disappeared behind the clouds. And then the storm
came—heavy rain speared by lightning. For more than an hour she tried
to hold her course as the little Vega was bounced around, but she had never
flown through skies so rough.

"If anyone finds the wreck," she wrote in her log, "know that the
nonsuccess was caused by my getting lost in a storm for an hour."

She decided to pull up above the storm clouds. But after a half hour
of climbing, the plane began to slow. There was slush on the window.

Ice. It was clinging to the plane, making it too heavy.

She knew she had to get into warmer air, so she headed down.

But with her broken altimeter she had no idea how far she was above the sea, until she saw whitecaps breaking right beneath her. If the sea had been smooth, she might never have realized she was about to hit water.

Then there were the flames. They were licking through a broken weld in the engine exhaust. Would the fire burn slowly and harmlessly until she could land, or would it flare up and spread? Amelia couldn't help wondering whether it would be better to drown or burn to death. At least, she thought, when daylight came, the flames wouldn't look so bright.

At last, dawn broke. But there was no land in sight. Amelia had been flying for thirteen hours on nothing but a few swallows of tomato juice. The plane was vibrating badly. A fuel gauge was leaking. She knew she had strayed off course, but where was she?

Finally she spotted land. It was the coast of Ireland. She followed a railroad track thinking it would lead to a town and an airfield, but no landing strip appeared. In the end, she came down in a long sloping meadow, scattering the cows in the fields.

She had done it.

Amelia poses with the Gallagher family, whose field she landed in on May 24, 1932, after completing her transatlantic flight.

Right: A ticker tape parade was held in Amelia's honor upon her return to the United States.

THE LAST FLIGHT

After Amelia completed her solo flight across the Atlantic, one ocean led to another. In 1935 she became the first woman to fly from Hawaii to California.

What would come next?

A trip around the world. Others had done it, but she would be the first woman, and the first to fly at the equator—the world's waistline.

Amelia had the plane for the job—a twin-engine all-metal Lockheed Electra. The cabin was filled with extra gas tanks to carry the plane long distances. It was equipped with an autopilot, two-way voice communication, and a radio direction finder that could point the way to a selected station within its range.

Amelia often said preparation was two-thirds of any venture, and that was certainly true now. Organizing her world flight took more than a year. This wasn't like driving across the country, where you could just set off and ask directions at the next gas station. She had to decide in advance at which airports she would land and learn about weather conditions during the times she would be in each place. She had to mark possible spots for emergency landings all along the way. Fuel and spare parts had to be shipped ahead to each airfield and several backup spots besides, and good mechanics had to be available to service the plane at every stop.

As she sat on her porch in California, studying maps and charts, her knowledge of geography grew from week to week while she planned her route from Oakland to Hawaii, and from there to Australia, Africa, Brazil, and back home. She tracked monsoon patterns in India and studied takeoff conditions in Africa. Planning the trip was such an adventure that she decided that one day she would write about "the fun of voyaging with maps—without ever leaving home."

More than seventy years after her disappearance, Amelia Earhart remains one of the most famous and iconic aviators in history.

Amelia clears the Golden Gate Bridge during her first
attempt to fly around the world, March 17, 1937.

"*Why* are you attempting this around-the-world flight?" people asked her again and again.

"Because I want to," she replied. But it was more than that. She wanted "shining adventure . . . new experiences." She wanted to learn more about flying, about people—and about herself. She believed that women should "do for themselves" what men had done, and even what they had not done.

On March 17, 1937, Amelia, along with two navigators and a technical adviser, took off from Oakland, California, in the late afternoon. San Francisco's brand-new Golden Gate Bridge glistened in the sunlight, looking like a shining "thread of steel" speckled with "tiny beetles crawling home." It seemed like a very good omen.

Amelia flew the Electra west, chasing the setting sun. She passed a passenger plane. She saw the planet Venus setting. She smelled coffee coming from the navigators' cabin as she flew through the night.

Daylight broke, and word came from the navigators that it was time to start down. It was a great relief to see the island of Oahu when she broke through the clouds. Hawaii is a small scattering of islands in the middle of the Pacific. She knew how easily she could have flown right past it.

They were delayed in Hawaii for two days, but Amelia didn't care. There were always delays in flying. Besides, this flight was not about speed. One day, she knew, people would fly around the globe so quickly it would take her breath away.

On March 20, as dawn crept over the hills above Pearl Harbor, Amelia began the second leg of her flight. The runway was wet from a light rain that had fallen overnight, and the plane was heavy with fuel, but it moved down the runway so easily that she thought she'd actually taken off.

Suddenly, she felt the plane pull to the right. She pulled back on the left throttle to reduce power on the left engine and managed to swing the

31

Amelia inspects her damaged Lockheed Electra after a takeoff accident at Luke Field, near Pearl Harbor, during her first attempt to fly around the world.

Electra around to the left. For a moment she thought she would be able to regain control and straighten, but the load was too heavy, and the plane just kept skidding around until it keeled over.

The landing gear was wiped off and one wing was damaged. Gas sprayed, but, to everyone's amazement, there was no fire.

"Of course, now you'll give up the trip?" someone asked after Amelia climbed out of the cockpit.

Amelia shook her head. "I think not," she said.

She would go back to the beginning. And start all over again.

Amelia takes off in her Lockheed Electra from Oakland, California, on her first attempt to fly around the world, March 1937.

Repairing the Electra was the least of her problems. The entire trip had to be planned again. Fuel, oil, spare parts, and mechanics had to be reassigned. Permission to land at foreign airports had to be reapplied for. More money—a lot more money—had to be raised to pay for it all.

She decided to reverse the direction of the original flight. After all, she told the press, the world was the same distance around, whether you flew from west to east or from east to west. And flying west to east meant she could test out her rebuilt plane over land before crossing water.

Amelia and her crew finally left Oakland for the second time on May 21. At Tucson, Arizona, the left engine burst into flames, though the fire was put out before it could spread. They flew into a sandstorm near El Paso, Texas.

Amelia says her final good-bye to George in Miami, Florida, on June 1, 1937.

Still, Amelia was happy. She was certain the worst was behind her.

This time she was flying with one navigator—Fred Noonan, one of the best in the business. At a stop on the north coast of Venezuela, they were served an elaborate luncheon right in the hangar, a wild orchid corsage pinned to her crumpled flying shirt. At every stop she and Fred were fed generously and given food for the flight. They had to be careful not to gain weight. Six extra pounds would mean leaving behind a gallon of precious fuel!

Above South America, she flew over jungle for the first time—nothing but solid forest for hundreds of miles. It was beautiful, but this was the worst place to be if she had to make an emergency landing. She knew of pilots who had pancaked onto the tightly packed treetops and then climbed down to the forest floor, but she didn't want to be one of them.

With so much to look at, it was sometimes hard to pay attention to what she called her "knitting"—the horizon and her instruments. Both she and Fred were so busy that they crossed the equator without noticing. Fred had even brought along a thermos of cold water to throw on Amelia to mark the occasion!

By June 7 they reached the edge of Brazil, and it was time to cross the Atlantic. At first the flight was uneventful. Then the heavens seemed to open as rain pounded the plane. Amelia could almost feel the weight of it on the roof of the cockpit. The rainwater mixed with the oil thrown back from the propellers, splashing the windows with brown muck. The gasoline fumes in the plane made her feel sick.

It was a great relief when they finally caught sight of the African coast, thirteen hours after leaving South America.

"Last week, home. Yesterday, South America. Today, Africa."

When she was a little girl, Amelia had taken many pretend journeys across this great continent of desert and jungle, mostly traveling on the back of an imaginary camel or elephant.

Now she was crossing the real Africa—in an airplane.

At each stop on her route she met with the same routine. The instant the plane landed, the doors were flung open and the cockpit was invaded by attendants with spray guns. They would give the plane—and Amelia and Fred—a vigorous disinfecting to kill any germs or disease-carrying insects.

Then mechanics got to work on the plane. Usually at least one part or system malfunctioned after several hours of flight. The Electra was treated like a prize race horse, every inch carefully examined before being scrubbed with soap and water and refueled.

Meanwhile, Amelia and Fred would have their papers checked by health and customs officials. Amelia would write up an account of the trip so far and send it home. Then she would be entertained by local dignitaries until she could politely get away. She would wash her clothes and fall into bed, exhausted. Often she returned to the airport before dawn for a test flight or early takeoff before the heat of the day set in.

Amelia dodged tornadoes and sandstorms as she made her way across Africa. She even flew past Timbuktu, the famed outpost at the edge of the Sahara where caravans

Amelia in the cockpit of her plane.

Around the World

1924 A team of American military pilots flies around the world in 175 days, covering a distance of about 27,000 miles. Of the four planes that start out, only two complete the trip.

1929 The German airship *Graf Zeppelin* flies around the world in twenty-one days, over a distance of 19,500 miles.

1931 American Wiley Post and his navigator fly a Lockheed Vega around the world in nine days, covering a distance of 15,494 miles. Two years later, Post repeats the feat, this time flying solo.

1937 Amelia Earhart attempts to be the first woman to fly around the globe at the equator—a distance of 29,000 miles. Her flight ends 7,000 miles short, after forty-three days.

1961 Russian Yuri Gagarin is the first human to orbit the earth, in 108 minutes.

Today, a commercial flight from Oakland to Honolulu takes about five and a half hours. In 1937 it took Amelia fifteen hours and forty-seven minutes to cover the same distance.

once brought gold, ivory, salt—and slaves—to be shipped down the Niger River to the sea.

Halfway across the continent, Lake Chad sprawled over thousands of square miles. Its shallow waters were peppered with dark islands outlined against the pale water. Some of the islands looked like "strange creatures . . . with lumpy paws and flat heads."

She saw real animals, too. Storks and cranes and blue herons feeding in the swamps. A herd of hippos mildly annoyed by the noise of the plane. From time to time she even saw evidence of human animals—a tent or two, or a wandering footpath, or a small cluster of thatched huts that looked like beehives. No crocodiles or elephants. But then, she couldn't spend too much time sightseeing. There were more than a hundred gadgets to pay attention to in the cockpit. She and Fred spent a lot of time trying to figure out exactly where they were.

At that time, much of central Africa had never been thoroughly mapped, and there were few landmarks to help them find their way. One part of the desert looked much the same as the next. There were few roads. Dotted red lines on the map traced trails that were invisible from the air. Curving lines marked rivers that existed only in the wet season.

Then there was the difficulty of flying in the extreme heat—something Amelia decided should be avoided by both humans and machines. By afternoon the metal plane was too hot to touch, and the cockpit was sweltering. More important, hot air was thin and lacked lifting power, and it was rougher to fly in.

Amelia sits in her Lockheed Electra.

Every place she went, she met with one surprise after another. So much of central Africa looked just like Arizona or New Mexico from the air that she practically had to pinch herself to remember that she wasn't flying over the canyons and mountains of the American Southwest. She was astonished to learn that the city of Khartoum in Northern Africa was laid out in the design of the British flag, the Union Jack. And she noticed that both the Blue Nile and the White Nile were, in fact, green, and the Red Sea was blue.

At last, on June 13, they came to the end of the continent. The city of Massawa, on the coast of the Red Sea, was 100 degrees the evening they arrived, but Amelia didn't mind. She'd soon be on her way again. She had made it over three continents. Her round-the-world flight was almost half over.

Two weeks later, Amelia was in Lae, New Guinea, on the edge of the Pacific Ocean. She had flown three-quarters of the way around the planet, and each day she had seen more of the world than most people see in their entire lives.

In central India she had flown through a sandstorm, where jagged mountain peaks poked up through the swirling sand like "sharks through a yellow sea." After that, they hit monsoon rains so thick it was like flying through a solid wall of water. The rain came down so hard that it beat patches of paint off the wings of the plane.

Amelia during a stop in Calcutta, India.

From the air she had gazed down at water buffalo, spooked by the sound of the plane, loping across soggy fields. She had seen farmers waving up at her from their green and tan fields, grass houses poking out of soil like mushrooms, a shimmering golden pagoda in Rangoon, and boats of every description floating in Singapore harbor like little water bugs.

Across Asia she had flown over rice paddies that looked like Christmas packages tied with brown ribbons that were actually irrigation ditches. They stretched up the sides of mountains in stairlike terraces. She had looked down at a mauve-colored sea, and at ribbons of beach so beautiful it was hard to pay attention to her instruments.

Now there was just one more ocean to cross—the mighty Pacific, the biggest one of all. For eighteen hours she and Fred would fly over open water until they reached Howland Island—a tiny speck in the middle of the South Pacific.

Amelia and Fred Noonan with a map of the Pacific showing the proposed route of the last flight they would make.

Where Are We?

In these days of satellites, the Global Positioning System, detailed maps, and computerized communication and navigation systems, it's easy to forget that in Amelia's day, pilots didn't always know where they were.

The most essential instrument was a compass, which was used to track a straight line to the destination. (When Amelia flew solo across the Atlantic, she simply followed her compass bearings east, knowing that she would hit Europe at some point.) Pilots also used known landmarks—mountains, towns, rivers, railway tracks—to stay on course, as well as radio contact with nearby ground stations to establish a plane's location.

But the slightest change in the wind could blow a plane off course. Early pilots studied clothes hanging on lines, smoke blowing from chimneys, or waves in the water to determine wind direction and strength.

Pilots fly the plane, but it's the navigators who help to keep them from getting lost. Navigators like Fred Noonan used instruments to measure the angle between the horizon and certain stars, planets, the sun, or the moon, which were known to be in specific positions at certain times of the day or night. Even for experienced navigators, reading the sky could be difficult, because things like the curve of the windshield, haze, or the slightest tip of the plane could cause false readings. Before takeoff it was also important to obtain an exact-to-the-second time check to set the instruments that determined longitude position. (An error of just four seconds could put a plane an entire mile off course.)

A sextant (shown here) is a tool that measures the elevation of an object in the sky, such as the moon or a star, in order to determine a navigational position.

Amelia stands on her Electra.

This would be the longest stretch yet—2,556 miles—and they would need all the fuel they could carry. The plane had never been heavier, even though Amelia and Fred had removed every spare ounce of weight, including flares and smoke bombs, spare parts, clothes, and tools.

At 10 o'clock on the morning of July 2, Amelia climbed on to the wing behind Fred and they lowered themselves through the hatch. Then she started the engines, using more power than usual to push the heavy plane to the end of the long runway.

She turned the plane around and pushed the throttles forward. The Electra lumbered down the grassy stretch, faster and faster.

Just fifty yards before the runway ended the plane finally left the ground and soared out over the water.

All she had to do now was cross one more ocean and get home safely.

Near Howland Island, a Coast Guard cutter waited for Amelia Earhart to arrive from New Guinea. All night the ship's radio operators had frantically tried to communicate with her. But messages from her plane had been choppy, and her voice had been drowned by static. More worrying, she had not acknowledged any of the ship's own messages, and there was no way of knowing whether she had even received them.

A welcome party scanned the horizon waiting for the sight and sound of a plane. The minutes and hours ticked by as Amelia's scheduled landing time came and went.

She never arrived.

The United States government immediately launched a massive search, at a cost of $4 million. For the next two weeks dozens of boats and planes crisscrossed 250,000 square miles of ocean looking for the lost Electra.

They found nothing.

EPILOGUE

The world found it difficult to accept that Amelia Earhart had simply vanished without a trace. And it wasn't long before rumors and theories began to fly.

During those years leading up to World War II, relations between Japan and America were tense. Some people said that Amelia was actually an American spy, and that her plane was shot down by the Japanese. Some claimed she had survived, secretly returned to America, and was alive and well in New Jersey.

Once the crazier ideas were discarded due to lack of evidence, two theories remained. Did she simply run out of gas and plunge into the ocean? Was the plane still lying somewhere on the bottom of the sea, preserved in the cold ocean depths?

Or did she continue to fly until, out of fuel, her plane crash-landed on the reef of a bigger island—Gardner Island (now called Nikumaroro)—that lay on her line of flight two hours to the south? Might she and Fred even have survived for a while as castaways? Could that explain the reports from people who claimed they had picked up radio signals from her for three nights after her disappearance?

In 2002 and 2006, two extensive searches of the ocean floor using the latest underwater exploration technologies failed to turn up any sign of the plane.

The shore of Nikumaroro Island, where some believe Amelia may have landed and survived for some time.

Left: Some theories suggest that, after running out of fuel, Amelia was forced to ditch her plane in the ocean.

43

Attempts to prove or disprove the landing on Nikumaroro have revealed more mysteries than they have solved. Three years after Amelia's last flight, several unusual items, including parts of a skeleton and a box for a sextant (a navigation instrument), were found on the island by a group of British explorers. Though the partial skeleton and sextant box have since gone missing, the bone measurements that were recorded were later determined to be those of a woman of Amelia's height and race, while the sextant box was found to be similar to one owned by Fred Noonan.

Later expeditions found other curious clues. In 1937 Nikumaroro was uninhabited, but settlers who arrived a short time later passed down stories of a wrecked plane

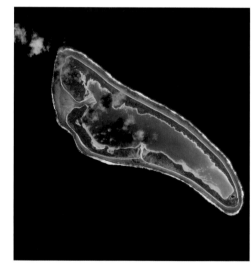

Above left: A map showing Saipan Island, where some believed Amelia, thought to be a spy, was imprisoned by the Japanese.

Left: An aerial view of Nikumaroro Island, where some believe Amelia landed successfully.

Right: A button and a zipper found on Nikumaroro Island that may have belonged to Amelia or Fred Noonan.

on the reef. Searchers have recently found combs, fishing tackle, decorations made of aircraft metal, and parts of an American-made shoe similar to those Amelia was wearing in a pre-takeoff photograph. The remains of campfires have also been found near the spot where the bones were discovered.

In these days of space missions, supersonic jets, and easy, fast air travel around the world, it's hard to believe that flying across an ocean was once considered such an amazing and dangerous accomplishment.

Yet when you take a closer look at Amelia's rickety first plane and remember how many things could and did go wrong during flights, it is clear that the pioneers of early aviation were brave indeed.

But Amelia Earhart did more than accomplish brave feats. She spoke out on behalf of women doing what they wanted, at a time when, as she put it, "girls don't" and "girls can't" influenced many young women in choosing a career. She had a mind of her own. Her quiet determination to lead her own life was remarkable then, and it still is now.

Perhaps her most important legacy is what she has to say to all of us—male and female—about having the courage to take on challenges and pursue a dream.

Think for yourself, she would say. Figure out what you love to do.

And then go out and do it.

Amelia in flight gear, circa 1920s.

"I want to do it because I want to do it. Women must try to do things as men have tried. When they fail, their failure must be but a challenge to others."

—*Amelia Earhart*

REFERENCES AND RESOURCES

This text is largely based on the writings of Amelia Earhart, including her three books: *20 Hrs., 40 Min.: Our Flight in the Friendship*, *The Fun of It*, and *Last Flight*. Phrases within quotation marks are taken directly from Amelia's works.

Books

Backus, Jean L. *Letters from Amelia.* Boston: Beacon, 1982.

Butler, Susan. *East to the Dawn: The Life of Amelia Earhart.* New York: Da Capo, 1999.

Cadogan, Mary. *Women with Wings: Female Flyers in Fact and Fiction.* London: Macmillan, 1992.

Earhart, Amelia. *The Fun of It: Random Records of My Own Flying and of Women in Aviation.* New York: Brewer, Warren & Putnam, 1932.

Earhart, Amelia. *Last Flight.* New York: Harcourt, Brace, 1937.

Earhart, Amelia. *20 Hrs., 40 Min.: Our Flight in the Friendship.* Washington, D.C.: National Geographic, 2003.

Gillespie, Ric. *Finding Amelia: The True Story of the Earhart Disappearance.* Annapolis: Naval Institute Press, 2006.

Long, Elgen M., and Marie K. Long. *Amelia Earhart: The Mystery Solved.* New York: Touchstone, 2001.

Putnam, George Palmer. *Soaring Wings: A Biography of Amelia Earhart.* New York: Harcourt, Brace, 1939.

Van Pelt, Lori. *Amelia Earhart: The Sky's No Limit.* New York: Tom Doherty Associates, 2005.

Ware, Susan. *Still Missing: Amelia Earhart and the Search for Modern Feminism.* New York: W.W. Norton, 1993.

Articles

Earhart, Amelia. "Flying the Atlantic." *American Magazine*, Vol. 114, August 1932, p. 72.

Earhart, Amelia. "My Flight from Hawaii." *National Geographic*, Vol. 67, No. 5, May 1935, pp. 593–609.

Holden, Alfred. "A Picture and a Thousand Words: Stunts made her famous but Amelia Earhart knew the future was in selling seats, not feats." *Toronto Star*, July 15, 2007.

Morrissey, Alisha. "Famous Flier Took Off from Newfoundland 75 Years Ago This Month." *The Telegram*, May 6, 2007.

"The Society's Special Medal Awarded to Amelia Earhart." *National Geographic*, Vol. 62, No. 3, September 1932, pp. 358–367.

Websites

Amelia Earhart, www.ameliaearhart.com.

"Commercial Flight in the 1930s." U.S. Centennial of Flight Commission, www.centennialofflight.gov/esay/Commercial_Aviation/passenger_xperience/Tran2.htm.

The Earhart Project, The International Group for Historic Aircraft Recovery (TIGHAR), www.tighar.org.

George Palmer Putnam Collection of Amelia Earhart Papers, ww.lib.purdue.edu.

Nauticos Corporation, www.nauticos.com.

The Ninety-Nines, www.ninety-nines.org.

SOURCE NOTES

Page 4. "Look, dear, it flies . . . for fifteen cents." Amelia Earhart, *Last Flight* (New York: Harcourt, Brace, 1937), p. 4.

Page 7. "first-time things." Amelia quoted in Susan Ware, *Still Missing: Amelia Earhart and the Search for Modern Feminism* (New York: W.W. Norton, 1993), p. 31.

Page 7. "rolly coaster." Amelia quoted in Jean L. Backus, *Letters from Amelia* (Boston: Beacon Press, 1982), p. 14.

Page 10. "peculiar things." *Last Flight*, p. 6.

Page 10. "Dad, you know . . . like to fly." *20 Hrs., 40 Mins.: Our Flight in the Friendship.* (Washington, D.C.: National Geographic, 2003), p. 11.

Page 12. "play around." Ibid., p. 20.

Page 13. "Suppose the fog . . . to the ground?" *20 Hrs., 40 Min.,* p. 30.

Page 13. "little crack ups." Amelia's letter to her mother, October 2, 1930, quoted in *Letters from Amelia*, p. 97.

Page 16. "cold lard with . . . floating in it." *The Fun of It: Random Records of My Own Flying and of Women in Aviation* (New York: Brewer, Warren & Putnam, 1932), p. 72.

Page 16. "voyage in the clouds." Ibid., p. 74.

Page 17. "shimmering veils." Ibid.

Page 17. "reared their heads like dragons." Ibid., p. 75.

Page 17. "gobs of mashed potatoes." Ibid., p. 76.

Page 17. "little lambs." *Last Flight*, p. 114.

Page 17. "white scrambled eggs." Ibid., p. 94.

Page 17. "gulping beauty." *20 Hrs., 40 Mins.*, p. 101.

Page 17. Quotes from children's letters quoted in *Last Flight*, p. 71.

Page 19. "sack of potatoes." Amelia's speech to the National Geographic Society on receiving the Society's Special Gold Medal. *National Geographic*, Vol. 62, No. 3, September 1932, p. 363.

Page 21. "You're saying . . . In everything." Alfred Holden, *Toronto Star*, July 15, 2007.

Page 25. "If anyone finds the wreck . . . in a storm for an hour." Amelia's flight log, Amelia Earhart collection, Purdue Libraries, www.purdue.edu/NNS/html4ever/ 020502.Earhart.donation.html.

Page 28. "the fun of voyaging . . . leaving home." *Last Flight*, p. 46.

Page 31. "*Why* are you . . . want to." Ibid., p. 48.

Page 31. "shining adventure . . . new experiences." Ibid.

Page 31. "do for themselves." Ibid.

Page 31. "thread of steel." Ibid., p. 52.

Page 31. "tiny beetles . . . home." Ibid.

Page 32. "Of course, now you'll give up . . . I think not." Ibid., p. 64.

Page 34. "knitting." Ibid., p. 180.

Page 35. "Last week, home . . . Africa." Ibid., p. 122.

Page 36. "strange creatures . . . flat heads." Ibid., p. 135.

Page 37. "sharks through a yellow sea." Ibid., p. 165.

Page 45. "girls don't . . . girls can't." *The Fun of It*, p. 144.

INDEX

Proofreader:
Judy Phillips

Indexer:
Anna Filippone

Historical Consultant:
Ric Gillespie

Initial Cover Visual Concept:
Blair Kerrigan / Glyphics

Produced by
MADISON PRESS BOOKS

Hannah Draper
Editor

Diana Sullada
Art Director and Designer

Sandra L. Hall
Production Manager

Susan Barrable
Vice President Finance and Production

Alison Maclean
Associate Publisher

Oliver Salzmann
President and Publisher